IS-860.C: The National Infrastructure Protection Plan, An Introduction

By

Fema

7/21/2015

Course Purpose

The purpose of this course is to raise awareness across the entire critical infrastructure community — including public and private sectors as well as government at all levels — of the National Infrastructure Protection Plan key concepts, core tenants and call to action and enhance knowledge to enable participants to apply these concepts to contribute to the security and resilience of critical infrastructure within their communities and areas of responsibility.

NIPP 2013, Partnering for Critical Infrastructure Security and Resilience guides efforts of stakeholders to enhance the security and resilience of critical infrastructure across the country in conjunction with national preparedness policy. It embraces a collaborative partnership built on comparative advantage; reinforces the importance of efficient information sharing grounded in appropriate legal protections, trusted relationships and enabling technologies; and focuses on risk management innovations and outcomes.

Course Objectives

In the lessons that follow, you will be introduced to the National Infrastructure Protection Plan (NIPP).

At the end of this course, you should be able to:

- Describe NIPP 2013 key concepts across the entire critical infrastructure community — including private sector and government at all levels.
- Describe the core tenets and the values and assumptions considered when planning for critical infrastructure security and resilience
- Identify activities critical partners may implement to achieve national goals aimed at enhancing critical infrastructure security and resilience put forward in the NIPP 2013 Call to Action
- Describe ways to apply these concepts to support security and resilience within your community or area of responsibility

This course is divided into four lessons.

NIPP Evolution

Today's unified approach to critical infrastructure security and resilience is guided by the requirements of Presidential Policy Directive 21: Critical Infrastructure Security and Resilience, issued by the President in 2013. While NIPP 2013 retains the basic building blocks of previous NIPPs, it also represents a significant evolution in several areas. For example, the updated Plan:

- Elevates security and resilience as the primary aim of critical infrastructure planning efforts;
- Calls for the establishment of national priorities—determined jointly by public and private sector partners—that will drive action at the national level and inform the development of goals and priorities at the sector, State, Local, Tribal, Territorial (SLTT) and regional levels; Focuses on establishing a process to set critical infrastructure national priorities determined jointly by the public and private sector;
- Directs joint decisionmaking by public and private sector partners initiated at the sector, SLTT and regional levels;
- Drives action at the federal level that in turn informs development of national goals and priorities
- Supports execution of the National Plan and achievement of the National Preparedness Goal at both the national and community levels, with focus on leveraging regional collaborative efforts; and
- Integrates cyber and physical security and resilience efforts into an enterprise approach to risk management.

Lesson 1 Overview

Examples of natural and manmade disasters, such as the Oklahoma City bombing, Hurricanes Katrina and Sandy, significant cyber-attacks and disruptions to the power grid, have impacted America's national and economic security as we are increasingly reliant on critical infrastructure, including cyber-based information systems. Regardless of what kind of hazard occurs within the Nation (natural or manmade), critical infrastructure is affected in some significant way (for example, disruption, damage, or destruction). When our critical infrastructure isn't fully functional, society suffers because the products and services provided by critical infrastructure underpin everything that we rely on to live our lives – food, water, healthcare, electricity, communications, transportation, etc.

By the end of this lesson you will be able to:

- Define critical infrastructure, security and resilience.
- Describe the unifying structure for integration of security and resilience efforts.
- Explain the importance of critical infrastructure partnerships.
- Recognize the seven Core Tenets and explain how they support critical infrastructure security and resilience

Audio Transcript

Critical infrastructure, such as water, energy, electricity and petroleum products, represent day-to-day goods and services that are a part of the life of every single American.

Critical infrastructure provides the foundation for the Nation's ability to maintain our way of life.

Protecting the critical infrastructure of the United States is essential to the Nation's security, public health and safety, economic vitality and way of life. Disruption of America's critical infrastructure could significantly interrupt the functioning of government and business alike and produce cascading effects far beyond the targeted sector and physical location of the incident. Direct terrorist attacks and natural, manmade, or technological hazards could produce catastrophic losses in terms of human casualties, property destruction and economic effects, as well as profound damage to public morale and confidence.

The National Infrastructure Protection Plan is the path forward toward building and enhancing protective measures for the critical infrastructure that sustain commerce and communities throughout the United States.

Critical Infrastructure

Our national well-being relies upon secure and resilient critical infrastructure—those assets, systems and networks that underpin American society.

NIPP 2013 guides the national effort to manage risk to the Nation's critical infrastructure. This national effort is shared by all levels of government and owners and operators of critical infrastructure. The Nation's critical infrastructure is largely owned and operated by the private sector; however, Federal, State, Local, Tribal and Territorial governments also own and operate critical infrastructure, as do foreign entities and companies.

Critical Infrastructure

Critical infrastructure includes systems and assets, whether physical or virtual, so vital to the United States that the incapacity or destruction of such systems and assets would have a debilitating impact on security, national economic security, national public health or safety, or any combination of those matters. Some examples of critical infrastructure include:

- Tunnels serving as a primary conduit for transportation, water, electric, communications and gas lines
- Supply lines bringing power, communications, food and water to a community
- Financial services underpinning our economic system

National Infrastructure Protection Plan (NIPP)

NIPP 2013 influences critical infrastructure security and resilience planning at all governmental and owner and operator levels by establishing a vision, mission and goals that are supported by a set of Core Tenets focused on risk management and partnership.

Building on the partnership and risk management framework introduced in 2006, the 2013 update is informed by changes in the risk, policy and operating environments and from experiences gained and lessons learned since the previous NIPP was issued.

The NIPP Mission and Vision

The strategic direction is driven by a common vision and mission; a Nation in which:

- Physical and cyber critical infrastructure remain secure and resilient;
- Essential services and products continue to be delivered in the face of incidents; and
- Communities and businesses adapt to changing conditions and withstand and rapidly recover from potential disruptions.

This vision complements and supports the President's priorities for national security, national preparedness and community resilience. Critical infrastructure partners collectively identify priorities, articulate clear goals, mitigate physical and cyber risks, measure progress and adapt based on feedback and the changing environment to strengthen security and resilience.

Click on the "Mission" and "Vision" boxes to read the NIPP Mission and Vision

The NIPP Mission

The NIPP Mission is "To strengthen the security and resilience of the Nation's critical infrastructure, by managing physical and cyber risks through the collaborative and integrated efforts of the critical infrastructure community."

The NIPP Vision

The NIPP Vision is "A Nation in which physical and cyber critical infrastructure remain secure and resilient, with vulnerabilities reduced, consequences minimized, threats identified and disrupted and response and recovery hastened."

Security and Resilience

Presidential Policy Directive 21 (PPD-21) defines security and resilience as follows:

Security: Reducing the risk to critical infrastructure by physical means or defens[ive] cyber measures to intrusions, attacks, or the effects of natural or manmade disasters.

Some examples of protective measures to increase critical infrastructure security include:

- Addressing threats and vulnerabilities
- Sharing accurate information and analysis on current and future risks
- Installing exterior locks and positioning bollards around an important building
- Properly marking and storing sensitive information

Resilience: The ability to prepare for and adapt to changing conditions and withstand and recover rapidly from disruptions; includes the ability to withstand and recover from deliberate attacks, accidents, or naturally occurring threats or incidents.

Some examples of preparedness efforts to increase critical infrastructure resilience include:

- Having accurate information and analysis about risk
- Planning for mitigation, response, and recovery activities
- Performing regular back-ups of information systems
- Pre-positioning emergency provisions in a separate location

NIPP 2013 Goals

The vision and mission depend on achieving five goals that strategically direct the focus of critical infrastructure activities.

The National Goals include:

1. Assess and analyze risks to critical infrastructure
2. Address the human, physical and cyber threat
3. Enhance security and resilience through advance planning
4. Share actionable and relevant information across the critical infrastructure community
5. Promote learning and adaptation

These goals will be augmented by the regular development of more specific risk management and capability enhancement priorities determined by the critical infrastructure partnership.

Click on the "Goals" box for complete descriptions of the five National Goals

National Infrastructure Protection Plan Goals

1. Assess and analyze threats to, vulnerabilities of and consequences to critical infrastructure to inform risk management activities;
2. Secure critical infrastructure against human, physical and cyber threats through sustainable efforts to reduce risk, while accounting for the costs and benefits of security investments;
3. Enhance critical infrastructure resilience by minimizing the adverse consequences of incidents through advance planning and mitigation efforts and employing effective responses to save lives and ensure the rapid recovery of essential services;
4. Share actionable and relevant information across the critical infrastructure community to build awareness and enable risk-informed decisionmaking; and
5. Promote learning and adaptation during and after exercises and incidents.

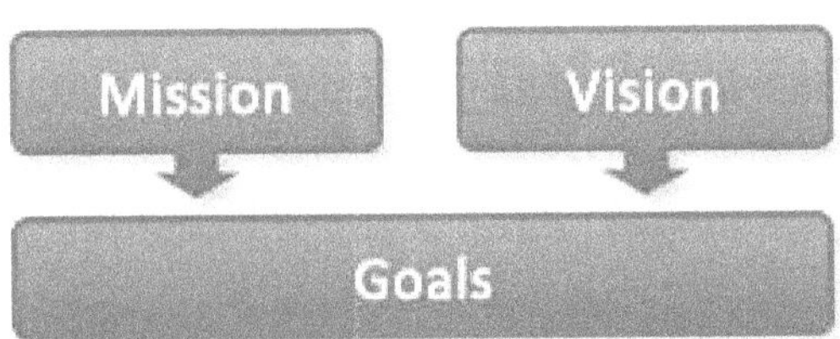

A Whole-Community Approach to Building and Sustaining Unity of Effort

Based on the vision, mission and goals, the critical infrastructure community works jointly to set specific national priorities, while considering resource availability, progress already made, known capability gaps and emerging risks. Jointly-developed priorities drive national action and are supplemented by sector, regional, State, Local, Tribal and Territorial priorities.

Performance measures will be set based on the goals and Joint National Priorities. National reporting mechanisms include measuring progress, which helps build a common understanding of the state of security and resilience efforts.

The interrelationship of these elements is depicted in the National Plan's approach to building and sustaining unity of effort.

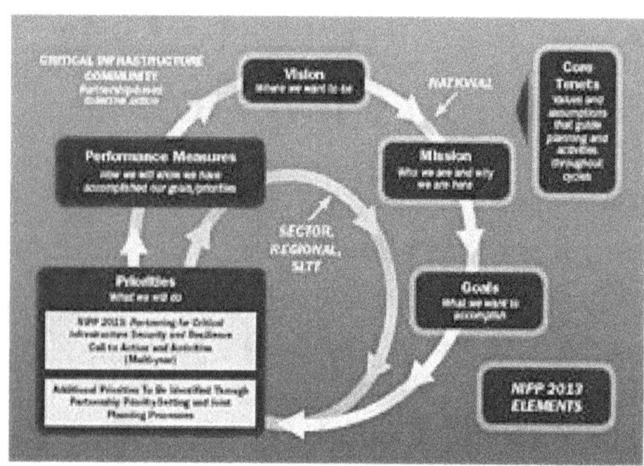

The National Plan's Approach to Building and Sustaining Unity of Effort

The critical infrastructure community works collaboratively to set specific national priorities, while considering resource availability, progress already made, known capability gaps and emerging risks.

Importance of Critical Infrastructure Partnerships

The community involved in managing risks to critical infrastructure is wide-ranging, composed of partnerships among private and public owners and operators; all levels of governments; regional entities; non-profit organizations; and academia. Secure and resilient critical infrastructure is achieved when the stakeholders leverage the full spectrum of capabilities, expertise and experience of their partners and share actionable and relevant information to effectively build situational awareness and effective risk-informed decisionmaking.

NIPP 2013 Supplements

NIPP 2013 is augmented by a series of supplements that serve as tools and resources that can be used to implement specific aspects of the Plan.

- Connecting to the National Infrastructure Coordinating Center (NICC) and the National Cybersecurity and Communications Integration Center (NCCIC)

- Executing a Critical Infrastructure Risk Management Approach
- Incorporating Resilience into Critical Infrastructure Projects
- National Protection and Programs Directorate Resources to Support Vulnerability Assessments

You will learn more about each of these supplements in later lessons.

The Core Tenets

Given the diverse roles and responsibilities across the infrastructure community, a proactive, collaborative and inclusive partnership among all levels of government and the private and non-profit sector is required to ensure optimal use of existing capabilities and to develop new ones. Additionally, infrastructure critical to the United States transcends national boundaries, requiring cross-border collaboration, mutual assistance and other cooperation.

The National Plan establishes seven Core Tenets, representing the values and assumptions the critical infrastructure community should consider when conducting security and resilience planning.

Select each core tenet to expand its NIPP 2013 description

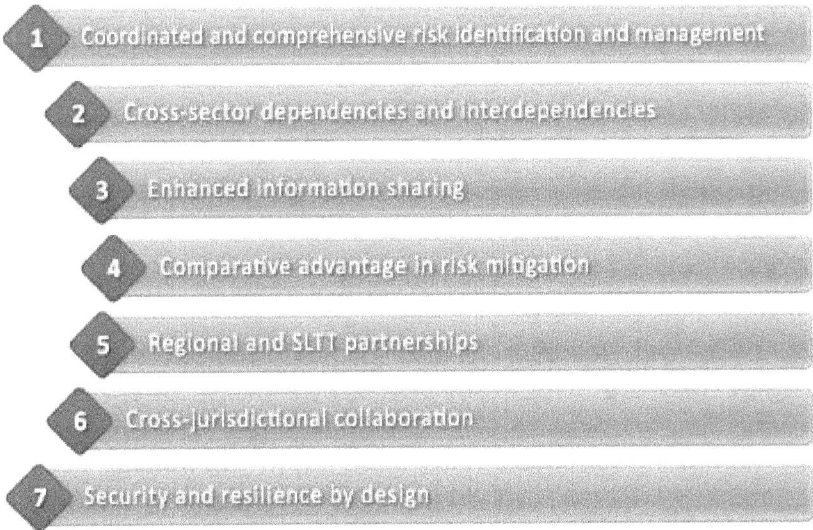

Core Tenet #1

Risk should be identified and managed in a coordinated and comprehensive way across the critical infrastructure community to enable the effective allocation of security and resilience resources.

Collaboratively managing risk requires sharing information (including smart practices), promoting more efficient and effective use of resources and minimizing duplication of effort. To ensure a comprehensive approach to risk management, the critical infrastructure community considers strategies to achieve risk mitigation, as well as other ways to address risk, including acceptance, avoidance, or transference.

Core Tenet #2

Understanding and addressing risks from cross-sector dependencies and interdependencies is essential to enhancing critical infrastructure security and resilience.

The way infrastructure sectors interact, including through reliance on shared information and communications technologies (e.g., cloud services), shapes how the Nation's critical infrastructure partners should collectively manage risk. It is important for the critical infrastructure community to understand and appropriately account for dependencies and interdependencies when managing risk. For example, all sectors rely on functions provided by energy, communications, transportation and water systems, among others.

Core Tenet #3

Gaining knowledge of infrastructure risk and interdependencies requires information sharing across the critical infrastructure community.

Critical infrastructure community members possess and produce diverse information useful to the enhancement of critical infrastructure security and resilience. Sharing and jointly planning based on this information is imperative to comprehensively address security and resilience in an increasingly interconnected environment. For that to happen, appropriate legal protections, trusted relationships, enabling technologies and consistent processes must be in place.

Core Tenet #4

The partnership approach to critical infrastructure security and resilience recognizes the unique perspectives and comparative advantages of the diverse critical infrastructure community.

The public-private partnership is central to maintaining critical infrastructure security and resilience. A well-functioning partnership depends on a set of attributes, including trust; a defined purpose for its activities; clearly articulated goals; measurable progress and outcomes to guide shared activities; leadership involvement; clear and frequent communication; and flexibility and adaptability. All levels of government and the private and nonprofit sectors bring unique expertise, capabilities and core competencies to the national effort. Recognizing the value of different perspectives helps the partnership more distinctly understand challenges and solutions related to critical infrastructure security and resilience.

Core Tenet #5

Regional and SLTT partnerships are crucial to developing shared perspectives on gaps and actions to improve critical infrastructure security and resilience.

The National Plan emphasizes partnering across institutions and geographic boundaries to achieve security and resilience. Risks often have local consequences, making it essential to execute initiatives on a regional scale in a way that complements and operationalizes the national effort. This requires locally based public, private and non-profit organizations to provide their perspectives in the assessment of risk and mitigation strategies.

Core Tenet #6

Infrastructure critical to the United States transcends national boundaries, requiring cross-border collaboration, mutual assistance and other cooperative agreements.

The United States benefits from and depends upon a global network of infrastructure.. The distributed nature and interconnectedness of these assets, systems and networks create a complex environment in which the risks the Nation faces are not distinctly contained within its borders. Services provided by critical infrastructure are often dependent on information gathered, stored, or processed in highly distributed locations. It is imperative that the government, private sector and international partners work collaboratively to fully understand supply chain vulnerabilities and to implement coordinated, not competing, global security and resilience measures. The National Plan is focused on domestic efforts, while recognizing the international aspects of the national approach.

Core Tenet #7

Security and resilience should be considered during the design of assets, systems and networks.

As critical infrastructure is built and refreshed, those involved in making design decisions, including those related to control systems, should consider the most effective and efficient ways to identify, deter, detect, disrupt and prepare for threats and hazards; mitigate vulnerabilities; and minimize consequences. This includes considering infrastructure resilience principles.

Lesson 1 Summary

In this lesson you learned to:

- Define critical infrastructure, security and resilience.
- Describe the unifying structure for integration of security and resilience efforts.
- Explain the importance of critical infrastructure partnerships.
- Recognize the seven Core Tenets and explain how they support critical infrastructure security and resilience.

Below are the NIPP 2013 resources referenced in this lesson for further review:

Lesson 2 Overview

When something threatens the homeland, it almost certainly threatens critical infrastructure and, due to the interconnectivity of all of our assets and systems, many other aspects of American life as well. NIPP 2013 is informed by changes in the risk, policy and operating environments, as well as experience gained and lessons learned from exercises and real-world events, such as Hurricane Sandy and various cyber incidents.

The update reflects the input and expertise of partners across the critical infrastructure community, including Federal, State, local, tribal and territorial governments; regional entities; private sector owners and operators; academic and non-profit organizations; and the public.

This lesson provides an overview of the critical infrastructure environment. By the end of this lesson, you will be able to:

- Describe the risk environment
- Identify dependencies and interdependencies across critical infrastructure systems
- Identify the relevant authorities and roles of:
    - The Department of Homeland Security (DHS).
    - Sector-Specific Agencies (SSAs).
    - Other Federal departments and agencies.
    - State, local, tribal and territorial jurisdictions.
    - Owners and operators.
- Discuss the importance of partnerships
- Describe the NIPP sector and cross-sector coordinating structure
- Describe how the NIPP fosters information sharing at all levels

The Risk Environment

Evolving Threats to Critical Infrastructure. Threats include extreme weather, accidents or technical failures, cyber threats, acts of terrorism, and pandemics. The risk environment is complex and uncertain; threats, vulnerabilities and consequences have all evolved over the last 10 years.

For example, due to the growing integration of information and communication technologies within operations and adversaries focusing on exploiting cyber vulnerabilities, critical infrastructure is increasingly exposed to cyber risks.

The Strategic National Risk Assessment (SNRA) defines numerous threats and hazards to homeland security. In addition to the known risks analyzed as part of the SNRA, the potential for interconnected events with unknown consequences adds uncertainty.

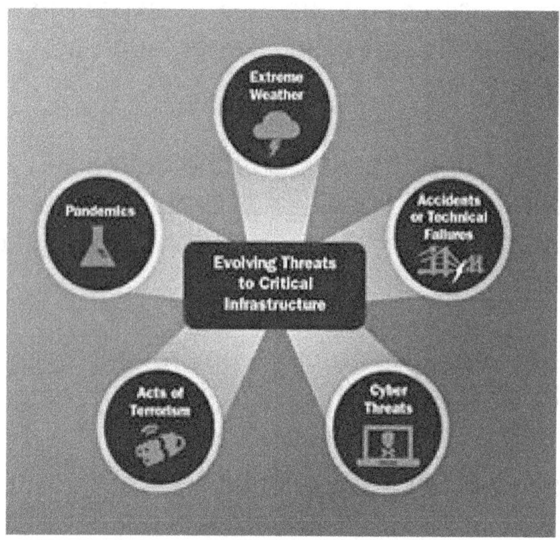

Threats that Pose the Greatest Risk to National Security

Critical assets, systems and networks face many broadly categorized threats including:

- **Natural**
    - Severe weather events and catastrophic natural disasters
    - Pandemic illnesses or other widespread health crises
- **Technological/Accidental**
    - Accidents or technical failures due to aging infrastructure
    - Chemical Substance Spill or Release
- **Adversarial/Human-caused**
    - Acts of terrorism
    - Cyber-attacks against data or physical assets
    - Other crimes intended to cause harm and disrupt essential services

You will learn more about these and other threats in Lesson 3

Complex Operating Environment

Collaborative planning and action is required due to the extent of interconnected infrastructure. The Nation's critical infrastructure has become much more interdependent, continuing to move from an operating environment characterized by disparate assets, systems and networks to one in which cloud computing, mobile devices and wireless connectivity have dramatically changed the way infrastructure is operated.

Interdependencies may be limited to small urban or rural areas or span vast regions, crossing jurisdictional and national boundaries, including infrastructure that require accurate and precise positioning, navigation and timing (PNT) data used in global positioning system (GPS), radio frequency identification (RFID), and global information systems (GIS) technology.

The nature of critical infrastructure ownership and operations is also distributed and the need for joint planning and investment to increase the security and resilience of critical infrastructure is becoming more common and necessary on the international level.

Interdependencies

Effective risk management requires an understanding of the criticality of assets, systems, and networks, as well as the associated dependencies and interdependencies of critical infrastructure.

Growing interdependencies, particularly reliance on information and communications technologies, have increased the potential vulnerabilities to physical and cyber threats and potential consequences resulting from the compromise of underlying systems or networks. The potential impacts increase with these interdependencies and the ability of a diverse set of threats to exploit them to cause harm and disrupt essential services.

Interdependencies affect all risk elements.
- Threat: Natural hazards such as extreme weather poses a significant risk to critical infrastructure, dependencies and interdependencies emerging from complex cyber capabilities and limitations can also pose a risk. Humans can also negatively impact critical infrastructure interdependencies through accidental, uninformed, or intentional activities to cause harm and disrupt essential services.
- Vulnerability: There is an expanded set of vulnerabilities due to interdependencies within an increasingly interconnected infrastructure.
- Consequence: Consequences such as accidents, technical failures, and compromise of interdependent systems or networks are greater due to

the potential for cascading impacts across multiple critical infrastructure assets, systems and networks.

Critical infrastructure is now increasingly exposed to cyber risks, which stems from growing operational integration of information and communications technologies, such as cloud computing, mobile devices and wireless connectivity, and an adversary focus on exploiting potential cyber vulnerabilities.

Interdependencies and dependencies help us consider second- and third-order effects. The focus on regional partnerships/initiatives is important because of the regionally interdependent nature of many critical infrastructure sectors.

Building on Homeland Security Strategies

Presidential Policy Directive 21 (PPD-21), Critical Infrastructure Security and Resilience explicitly calls for the development of an updated national plan.

In July of 2016, Presidential Policy Directive 41: United States Cyber Incident Coordination Policy (PPD-41) was issued by President Barack Obama. This new directive sets forth principles governing the Federal Government's response to any cyber incidents and provides architecture for coordinating the response to significant cyber incidents. Specifically, the PPD establishes three Federal lines of effort for any cyber incident: threat response; asset response; and intelligence support and related activities. This PPD also establishes lead Federal agencies responsibilities for coordinating Federal responses to significant cyber incidents.

The NIPP fulfills this requirement as it formalizes and strengthens existing critical infrastructure partnerships, and creates the baseline for how the public and private sectors will work together.

In addition, the National Plan fulfills requirements in Homeland Security Act of 2002 and is consistent with Executive Order 13636: Improving Critical Infrastructure Cybersecurity (2013); and aligns with the goal of Presidential Policy Directive 8 (PPD-8): National Preparedness (2011) and its supporting National Planning Frameworks: and two other policy documents: the President's Climate Action Plan (2013); and the National Strategy for Information Sharing and Safeguarding (2013).

Click on each document title for more information.

Risk in the Context of National Preparedness

The figure illustrates the relationship between the five National Preparedness mission areas (Prevent, Protect, Mitigate, Respond, and Recover) and the elements of risk (threat, vulnerability, and consequence). The graph shows that prevention activities are most closely associated with efforts to address threats; protection activities generally address vulnerabilities; and response and recovery activities help to minimize consequences. Mitigation activities span the entire risk spectrum. The graph also shows that prevention and protection efforts are most often associated with security, while response and recovery efforts are more closely linked to resilience. Mitigation activities can be associated with both security and resilience. The figure includes a quote from the National Preparedness Goal of 2011, which reads: 'A secure and resilient Nation maintains the capabilities required across the whole community to prevent, protect against, mitigate, respond to, and recover from the threats and hazards that pose the greatest risk.'

PPD-8 creates the National Preparedness Goal and System which describe five mission areas that provide a useful framework for considering risk management investments. The graphic titled "Critical Infrastructure Risk in the Context of National Preparedness" illustrates the relationship of the national preparedness mission areas to the elements of risk.

- **Prevention** activities are most closely associated with efforts to address threats;
- **Protection** efforts generally address vulnerabilities; and
- **Response** and **Recovery** efforts help minimize consequences.
- **Mitigation** efforts transcend the entire threat, vulnerability and consequence spectrum.

The National Preparedness Goal also establishes 31 core capabilities that support the five national preparedness mission areas. The NIPP is aligned with PPD-8 and the PPD-8 mission areas are central to a comprehensive approach for enhancing national preparedness and critical infrastructure risk management activities. The development of these capabilities contributes to achieving secure and resilient critical infrastructure; additionally, the capabilities can be applied to identify risk management activities.

Such efforts are enhanced when critical infrastructure risks are considered as part of setting capability targets.

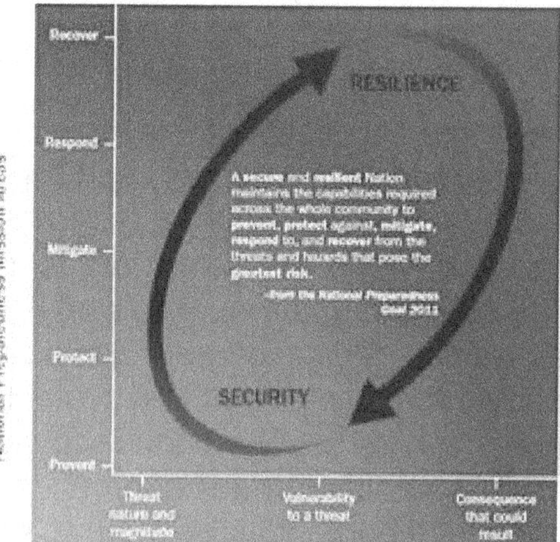

An Integrated Plan

The NIPP was created to complement, not replace, the Homeland Security plans and strategies, business continuity plans, preparedness strategies and security policies already developed by the critical infrastructure and first responders communities.

These existing private sector and government plans and strategies address an all-hazards approach and serve to broaden resilience and security measures for a variety of natural and manmade incidents.

Processes outlined in the NIPP are designed to enhance coordination, cooperation and collaboration among critical infrastructure partners within cross-sectors to synchronize related efforts and avoid duplicative or unnecessarily costly risk management requirements.

Critical Infrastructure Risk in the Context of National Preparedness

Critical infrastructure security and resilience rely on all of the preparedness mission areas.

In a crosswalk to the elements of Risk: Threat, Vulnerability and Consequences,

- Prevention activities are most closely associated with efforts to address Threats;
- Protection efforts generally address Vulnerabilities; and
- Response and Recovery efforts help minimize Consequences.

- Mitigation efforts transcend the entire Threat, Vulnerability and Consequence spectrum.

These five mission areas, as described in the National Preparedness Goal and System, provide a useful framework for considering risk management investments.

Critical Infrastructure Partnerships

The NIPP partnership model provides a framework used to promote and facilitate sector and cross-sector planning, coordination, collaboration and information sharing for security and resilience, involving all levels of government and private sector entities.

As the nature of the critical infrastructure risk environment precludes any one entity from managing risks entirely on its own, partners benefit from access to knowledge and capabilities that would otherwise be unavailable to them.

Many critical infrastructure sectors have worked to establish stable and representative partnerships, managing transitions in leadership and broadening the range of members and skill sets needed to accomplish collective goals.

Through trusted relationships and information sharing, Federal agencies gain a better understanding of the risks and preparedness posture associated with critical infrastructure. This allows entities to make more informed decisions when identifying and addressing national critical infrastructure priorities.

Critical Infrastructure Partners

The NIPP defines critical infrastructure partners as those Federal, State, regional, territorial, local, or tribal government entities, private sector owners and operators and representative organizations, academic and professional entities and certain not-for-profit and private volunteer organizations that share in the responsibility for protecting the Nation's critical infrastructure.

A National Partnership Model

PPD-21 describes critical infrastructure security and resilience as a shared responsibility between governments at all levels and the private sector and calls for an evaluation of the existing public-private partnership, which identified the attributes of effective partnerships.

NIPP 2013 expands on this concept by acknowledging the differing perspectives that drive government and industry partners who work collaboratively toward shared goals.

The partnership approach to critical infrastructure security and resilience recognizes the unique perspectives and comparative advantages of the diverse critical infrastructure community.

The NIPP is designed to be implemented using organizational structures and partnerships committed to sharing and protecting the information needed to achieve the NIPP goal and supporting objectives.

The NIPP Sector Partnership Model

The sector partnership model is a representation of how the private sector and government serve as equal partners to accomplish the infrastructure security and resilience mission.

Through the partnership model and its forums, the private sector and government conduct planning and share information, manage risk and ensure continuous improvement.

Appendix A of the NIPP further describes the functions of the partnership structures, as well as additional structures that support national critical infrastructure security and resilience.

Coordination Mechanisms

The sector and cross-sector partnership approach is designed to be scalable and allow individual owners and operators of critical infrastructure and other stakeholders across the country to participate.

It is intended to promote consistency of process to enable efficient collaboration between disparate parts of the critical infrastructure community, while allowing for the use of other viable partnership structures and planning processes.

This concept has proved successful and can be leveraged at the State, local, tribal and territorial levels as well as within and across regions to

- Build, form, or expand existing networks;
- Identify proven practices;
- Adapt to or adopt lessons learned; and

- Leverage practices, processes, or plans as appropriate.

The blue vertical arrows of the National Partnership Model represent collaborative structures through which representative groups from Federal, State, local, tribal and territorial governments and the private sector can collaborate and develop consensus approaches to critical infrastructure security and resilience.

The sector partnership model facilitates the integration of all partners into critical infrastructure planning and operational activities.

Sector and Cross-sector Council Structures Incclude:

Critical Infrastructure Partnership Advisory Council

Many of the sector and cross-sector council structures take advantage of the Critical Infrastructure Partnership Advisory Council (CIPAC) legal framework.

Established in 2006 by the Secretary of Homeland Security to facilitate effective coordination between federal infrastructure protection programs with the infrastructure protection activities of the private sector and of state, local, territorial and tribal governments, CIPAC allows members of the SCCs and GCCs to engage in joint critical infrastructure security-related discussions and participate in a broad spectrum of activities.

While operating under the CIPAC framework, the public-private critical infrastructure partnership meetings are exempt from the Federal Advisory Committee Act (FACA), allowing partners to engage in frank or sensitive dialogue.

The Value Proposition

Finding the appropriate value proposition among partners requires understanding these differing perspectives and how they may affect efforts to set joint priorities. Within these parameters, critical infrastructure security and resilience depend on applying risk management practices of both industry and government, coupled with available resources and incentives, to guide and sustain efforts.

NIPP 2013 promotes the concept of comparative advantage, where the unique skills and resources of individual partners are leveraged and brought to bear in a collective manner to reduce critical infrastructure risk.

Appendix B of the NIPP lists roles, responsibilities and capabilities of critical infrastructure partners and stakeholders

Value Proposition for Critical Infrastructure Private Sector Partners

Many industries justify their critical infrastructure security and resilience efforts based on corporate business needs.

Government can support these private sector efforts and assist in broad-scale preparedness through activities such as:

- Providing owners and operators with timely, analytical, accurate and useful information on threats to critical infrastructure.
- Ensuring that industry is engaged as early as possible in the development of policies and initiatives related to NIPP implementation.
- Articulating to corporate leaders the business and national security benefits of investing in security measures that exceed their business case.
- Creating an environment that encourages and supports incentives and encourages companies to voluntarily adopt widely accepted security practices.
- Working with industry to develop and clearly prioritize key missions and enable the protection and/or restoration of related critical infrastructure.
- Providing support for R&D initiatives that are needed to enhance future critical infrastructure security and resilience efforts.
- Providing the resources to enable cross-sector interdependency studies, exercises, symposiums, training sessions and computer modeling; and otherwise support business continuity planning.
- Enabling time-sensitive information sharing and restoration and recovery support to priority critical infrastructure facilities and services during emerging threat and incident management situations.

Roles, Responsibilities and Capabilities of Critical Infrastructure Partners and Stakeholders

PPD-21 states, "An effective national effort to strengthen critical infrastructure security and resilience must be guided by a national plan that identifies roles and responsibilities and is informed by the expertise, experience, capabilities and responsibilities of the SSAs, other Federal departments and agencies with critical infrastructure roles, SLTT entities and critical infrastructure owners and operators."

PPD-41 also recognizes the shared responsibility for cybersecurity, response activities have been outlined under PPD-41 into three concurrent lines of effort: threat response, asset response, intelligence support and related activities. These concurrent lines of effort provide a foundation for harmonizing various response efforts and fostering coordination and unity of effort before, during, and after any cyber incident response.

NIPP 2013 Appendix B includes the roles, responsibilities and capabilities of critical infrastructure partners and stakeholders including those Federal Roles as prescribed in PPD-21 as well as those for State, Local, Tribal and Territorial governments as well as critical infrastructure owners and operators, advisory councils and committees and academic and research organizations.

This section of the lesson provides an overview of partner and stakeholder roles.

Secretary of Homeland Security

The Secretary of Homeland Security provides strategic guidance, promotes a national unity of effort and coordinates the overall Federal effort to promote the security and resilience of the Nation's critical infrastructure.

As the principal Federal official for domestic incident management, the Secretary for Homeland Security coordinates Federal preparedness activities in alignment with PPD-8, including coordinating Federal Government responses to significant cyber or physical incidents affecting critical infrastructure (consistent with statutory authorities).

The Secretary of Homeland Security coordinates with other relevant members of the Executive Branch, as appropriate, to support a single, comprehensive approach to domestic incident management so all levels of government across the Nation have the capability to work efficiently and effectively together, using a national approach to domestic incident management.

Additional DHS roles and responsibilities include, as appropriate:

- Establish and maintain a comprehensive, multi-tiered and dynamic information-sharing network to provide timely and actionable threat information, assessments and warnings to public and private sector partners;
- Sponsor critical infrastructure security and resilience-related research and development, demonstration projects and pilot programs;
- Conduct modeling and simulations with SSAs to analyze sector, cross-sector and regional dependencies and interdependencies (including cyber dependencies) and share the results with critical infrastructure partners, as appropriate;
- Document and apply lessons learned from exercises, actual incidents and pre-disaster mitigation efforts to critical infrastructure security and resilience activities; and
- Evaluate the need for and coordinate the security and resilience of additional critical infrastructure categories over time.

Sector-Specific Agencies

Presidential Policy Directive 21 (PPD-21) designated responsibility to various Federal Government departments and agencies to serve as Sector-Specific Agencies (SSAs) for each of the critical infrastructure sectors and established criteria for identifying additional sectors.

The National Strategy for Information Sharing and Safeguarding (NSISS) identifies, as one of 16 national priorities, the need to establish "information-sharing processes and sector-specific protocols with private sector partners, to improve information quality and timeliness and secure the Nation's infrastructure."

SSAs are responsible for working with the Department of Homeland Security to implement the NIPP sector partnership model and risk management framework; develop protective programs, resilience strategies and related requirements; and provide sector-level critical infrastructure protection guidance.

DHS, in close collaboration with the SSAs, is responsible for overall coordination of the NIPP partnership organization and information-sharing network.

The National Goals are supported by objectives and priorities developed collaboratively at the sector level, which may be articulated in Sector-Specific

Plans (SSPs) and serve as targets for joint planning among SSAs and their sector partners in government and the private sector.

Other Federal Agencies

As stated in PPD-21, Federal departments and agencies provide timely information to the Secretary of Homeland Security and the national critical infrastructure centers necessary to support cross-sector analysis and inform the situational awareness capability for critical infrastructure; the centers in turn share the information back with the appropriate critical infrastructure partners.

Federal departments and agencies that are not designated as SSAs, but have unique responsibilities, functions, or expertise in a particular critical infrastructure sector (such as GCC members) assist in identifying and assessing high-consequence critical infrastructure and collaborate with relevant partners to share security and resilience-related information within the sector, as appropriate.

Presidential Policy Directive 41 (PPD-41) establishes a coordination structure in order to facilitate a more unified response for handling significant cyber incidents.

- National Policy Level Coordination
- Operational Level Coordination
- Sector Coordination

In the event of a significant cyber incident, Federal lead agency responsibilities are identified as follows for coordination:

- Threat Response - The Department of Justice, acting through the Federal Bureau of Investigation and the National Cyber Investigative Joint Task Force, will serve as the lead Federal agency for threat response.
- Asset Response - DHS, acting through the National Cybersecurity and Communications Integration Center (NCCIC), will serve as the lead Federal agency for asset response activities.
- Intelligence Support - The office of the Director of National Intelligence, through the Cyber Threat Intelligence Integration Center, will serve as the lead Federal agency for intelligence support and related activities.

More information on capabilities of partners is provided in Appendix B of the NIPP

Critical Infrastructure Owners and Operators

Critical infrastructure owners and operators in the public and private sector develop and implement security and resilience programs for the critical infrastructure under their control, while taking into consideration the public good as well. Owners and operators take action to support risk management planning and investments in security as a necessary component of prudent business planning and operations.

In today's risk environment, these activities generally include
- Reassessing and adjusting business continuity and emergency management plans,
- Building increased resilience and redundancy into business processes and systems,
- Protecting facilities against physical and cyber-attacks,
- Reducing the vulnerability to natural disasters,
- Guarding against insider threats and
- Increasing coordination with external organizations to avoid or minimize the impact on surrounding communities or other industry partners.

Owners and Operators Critical Infrastructure Security-Related Activities

For many private sector enterprises, the level of investment in security reflects risk-versus-consequence tradeoffs that are based on two factors:

1. That which is known about the risk environment

- The Federal Government is uniquely positioned to help inform investment decisions and operational planning.
- Owners and operators may look to the government and information sharing and analysis organizations like Information Sharing and Analysis Centers (ISACs) as a source of security-related best practices and for attack or natural hazard indications, warnings and threat assessments.

2. That which is economically justifiable and sustainable in a competitive marketplace or within resource constraints.

- Owners and operators may rely on government entities or participate in collective efforts with other owners and operators to address risks outside of their property or in situations in which the current threat exceeds an enterprise's capability to protect itself or requires an unreasonable level of additional investment to mitigate risk.

- In this situation, public and private sector partners at all levels collaborate to address the security and resilience of national-level critical infrastructure, provide timely warnings and promote an environment in which critical infrastructure owners and operators can carry out their specific responsibilities.

Critical infrastructure owners and operators participate in many cyber risk mitigation activities including

- Cybersecurity information-sharing efforts (e.g., sector-specific cyber working groups, the Cross-Sector Cybersecurity Working Group and the Industrial Control Systems Joint Working Group),
- Cyber risk assessments,
- Cybersecurity exercises,
- Cyber incident response and recovery efforts and
- Cyber metrics development.

The roles of specific owners and operators vary widely within and across sectors. Some sectors have statutory and regulatory frameworks that affect private sector security operations within the sector; however, most are guided by a voluntary focus on security and resilience or adherence to industry-promoted best practices.

Critical infrastructure owners and operators may contribute to national critical infrastructure security and resilience efforts through a range of activities. These activities may include but are not limited to:

- Performing critical infrastructure risk assessments;
- Understanding dependencies and interdependencies;
- Developing and coordinating emergency response plans with appropriate Federal and SLTT government authorities;
- Establishing continuity plans and programs that facilitate the performance of lifeline functions during an incident;
- Participating in critical infrastructure-focused training and exercise activities with public and private sector partners; and
- Contributing technical expertise to the critical infrastructure security and resilience efforts of DHS and the SSAs.

State, Local, Tribal and Territorial Governments

State, local, tribal and territorial governments are responsible for implementing the homeland security mission, protecting public safety and welfare and ensuring the provision of essential services to communities and industries within their jurisdictions.

States and territorial governments also:

- Serve as crucial coordination hubs, bringing together preparedness authorities; capabilities; and resources.
- Coordinate requests for Federal assistance when the threat or incident situation exceeds jurisdictional capabilities.
- Develop and implement statewide/regional critical infrastructure security and resilience programs that reflect the full range of NIPP-related activities.

Facilitate the information-sharing process. States receive critical infrastructure information from the Federal Government to support national and State critical infrastructure security and resilience programs.

State and Territorial Government Critical Infrastructure Security-Related Activities

- Establish partnerships and facilitate coordinated information sharing;
- Enable planning and preparedness for their jurisdictions;
- Serve as crucial coordination hubs;
- Receive critical infrastructure information from the Federal Government to support national and State critical infrastructure security and resilience programs;
- Provide information to DHS, regarding State or territorial priorities, requirements and critical infrastructure-related funding needs;
- Work with State and territorial-level sector-specific agencies to support the vision, mission and goals of this National Plan within those sectors, as appropriate;
- Engage subject matter experts at the sector level to assist with this effort;
- Address all relevant aspects of critical infrastructure security and resilience;
- Leverage support from homeland security assistance programs that apply across the homeland security mission area and;
- Reflect priority activities in their strategies to ensure that resources are effectively allocated.

Effective Statewide and regional critical infrastructure security and resilience efforts should be integrated into the overarching homeland security program framework at the State or territorial level to ensure that efforts are synchronized and mutually supportive.

Critical infrastructure security and resilience at the State or territorial level must cut across all sectors present within the jurisdiction and support national, State and local priorities. The program also should explicitly address unique geographical issues, including trans-border concerns, as well as interdependencies among sectors and jurisdictions within those geographical boundaries.

Regional Partners

Regional partnerships include a variety of public-private sector initiatives that cross jurisdictional and/or sector boundaries and focus on homeland security preparedness within or serving the population of a defined geographical area.

Specific regional initiatives range in scope from organizations that include multiple jurisdictions and industry partners within a single State, tribe, or territory to groups that involve jurisdictions and enterprises across State, tribal, territorial and international borders.

Regionally-based Partnership Activities

State governments can also collaborate through the adoption of interstate compacts to formalize regionally-based partnerships.

Partners in regional initiatives are encouraged to capitalize on the expertise and relationships to:

- Promote collaboration among partners;
- Facilitate education and awareness ;
- Participate in regional exercise and training programs, including a focus on collaboration across jurisdictional and sector boundaries;
- Support threat-initiated and ongoing operations-based activities to enhance security and resilience and to support mitigation, response and recovery;
- Work with SLTT and international governments and the private sector to evaluate regional and cross-sector critical infrastructure interdependencies, including cyber considerations;
- Conduct appropriate regional planning efforts and undertake appropriate partnership agreements;
- Facilitate information sharing and data collection between and among regional initiative members and external partners;
- Share information on progress and critical infrastructure security and resilience requirements with DHS, the SSAs, State and local governments and other critical infrastructure partners, as appropriate; and

- Participate in the critical infrastructure partnership.

Regional Partners: Best Practices

Regional partners are able to connect on critical infrastructure security and resilience issues through entities other than the national-level partnership and government-led models. One mechanism is through regional partnership coalitions, such as ChicagoFIRST.

ChicagoFIRST is a member of the Regional Consortium Coordinating Council and has a membership that is primarily from the Banking and Finance Sector. ChicagoFIRST collaborates with the City of Chicago, the State of Illinois, the U.S. Department of the Treasury, DHS and other critical sectors on disaster preparedness and business continuity issues. The members of ChicagoFIRST are private sector firms.

One of its most critical achievements is the establishment and maintenance of relationships between the members and government. ChicagoFIRST acts as a conduit for information for its members and coordinates with government at all levels to provide its member firms with a means to address industry issues and gather information for their own crisis response.

State and Regionally Based Boards, Commissions, Authorities, Councils and Other Entities

An array of boards, commissions, authorities, councils and other entities at the State, local, tribal and regional levels perform regulatory, advisory, policy, or business oversight functions related to various aspects of critical infrastructure operations and security within and across sectors and jurisdictions.

Some of these entities are established through State- or local-level executive or legislative mandates with elected, appointed, or voluntary membership.

These groups include, but are not limited to, transportation authorities, public utility commissions, water and sewer boards, park commissions, housing authorities, public health agencies and many others.

These entities may serve as State-level sector-specific agencies and contribute expertise, assist with regulatory authorities, or help facilitate investment decisions related to critical infrastructure security and resilience efforts within a given jurisdiction or geographic region.

Commissions: Best Practices

Public utility commissions are responsible for electricity, gas and telecommunications infrastructures and, in some cases, water, wastewater/sewage and certain aspects of transportation. Working together, public utility commissions are able to address issues of mutual concern based on the interdependencies between the water, communications and energy infrastructures by:

- Creating networks among utility regulators and other government and private sector entities to address cross-sector issues.
- Recommending strategies to facilitate information sharing.
- Recommending cost-effective solutions to cost-recovery issues associated with protecting key water, gas, communications and energy infrastructures.
- Identifying and prioritizing issues, researching best practices and disseminating information to partners and affiliates.

Local Governments

Local governments represent the frontlines for homeland security and, more specifically, for critical infrastructure security and implementation of the NIPP.

Local governments:

- Provide critical public services and functions in conjunction with private sector owners and operators.
- In some sectors, local government entities own and operate critical infrastructure such as water, storm water and electric utilities.
- Drive emergency preparedness, as well as local participation in NIPP and SSP implementation, across a variety of jurisdictional partners.

Local Government Critical Infrastructure Security and Resilience-Related Activities

Critical infrastructure protection focus at the local level should include, but is not limited to:

- Acting as a focal point for and promoting the coordination of protective and emergency response activities, preparedness programs and resource support among local agencies, businesses and citizens;
- Developing a consistent approach at the local level to critical infrastructure identification, risk determination, mitigation planning and prioritized security investment and exercising preparedness among all relevant partners within the jurisdiction;
- Identifying, implementing and monitoring a risk management plan and taking corrective actions, as appropriate;
- Participating in significant national, State, local and regional education and awareness programs to encourage appropriate management and security of cyber systems;
- Facilitating the exchange of security information, including threat assessments, attack indications and warnings and advisories, among partners within the jurisdiction;
- Participating in the NIPP sector partnership model, including GCCs, SCCs, SLTTGCC and other critical infrastructure structures relevant to the given jurisdiction;
- Ensuring that funding priorities are addressed and that resources are allocated efficiently and effectively to achieve the critical infrastructure security and resilience mission in accordance with relevant plans and strategies;
- Establishing continuity plans and programs that facilitate the performance of critical functions during an emergency or until normal operations can be resumed;
- Sharing with partners, as appropriate, critical infrastructure information deemed to be critical from the local perspective to enable prioritized protection and restoration of critical public services, facilities, utilities and processes within the jurisdiction;
- Addressing unique geographical issues, including trans-border concerns, dependencies and interdependencies among agencies and enterprises within the jurisdiction;
- Identifying and implementing plans and processes for step-ups in protective measures that align to all-hazards warnings; specific threats, as appropriate; and each level of the HSAS;
- Documenting lessons learned from pre-disaster mitigation efforts, exercises and actual incidents and applying that learning, where applicable, to the critical infrastructure security context; and

- Conducting critical infrastructure security and resilience public awareness activities.

Advisory Councils

Advisory councils:
- Provide advice, recommendations and expertise to the government regarding critical infrastructure security policy and activities.
- Help enhance public-private partnerships and information sharing.
- Often provide an additional mechanism to engage with a pre-existing group of private sector leaders to obtain feedback on critical infrastructure policy and programs and
- Make suggestions to increase the efficiency and effectiveness of specific government programs.

Examples of critical infrastructure security and resilience-related advisory councils and their associated roles:
- **Homeland Security Advisory Council:** Provides advice and recommendations to the Secretary of Homeland Security on relevant issues; council members, appointed by the DHS Secretary, include experts from State and local governments, public safety, security and first-responder communities, academia and the private sector.
- **Private Sector Senior Advisory Committee:** Subcommittee of HSAC that provides the council with expert advice from leaders in the private sector.
- **National Infrastructure Advisory Council:** Provides the President, through the Secretary of Homeland Security, with advice on the security of physical and cyber systems across all critical infrastructure sectors; comprises up to 30 members appointed by the President, which are selected from the private sector, academia and State and local governments. The council was established (and amended) under Executive Orders 13231, 13286, 13385 and 13652.
- **National Security Telecommunications Advisory Committee:** Provides industry-based advice and expertise to the President on issues and problems related to implementing National Security and Emergency Preparedness communications policy; comprises up to 30 industry chief executives representing the major communications and network service providers and information technology, finance and aerospace companies.

Academia and Research Centers

The academic and research communities play an important role in enabling national-level critical infrastructure security and resilience, including:

- Establishing Centers of Excellence (i.e., university-based partnerships or federally funded R&D centers) to provide independent analysis of critical infrastructure security and resilience issues;
- Supporting the research, development, testing, evaluation and deployment of security and resilience technologies;
- Supporting development and implementation of concepts, architectures and technical strategies associated with critical infrastructure security and resilience;
- Analyzing, developing and sharing best practices related to critical infrastructure prioritization, security and resilience efforts;
- Researching and providing innovative thinking and perspective on threats and the behavioral aspects of terrorism and criminal activity;
- Preparing or disseminating guidelines and descriptions of best practices for physical and cyber security;
- Developing and providing suitable all-hazards risk analysis and risk management courses for critical infrastructure security and resilience professionals;
- Establishing undergraduate and graduate curricula and degree programs;
- Conducting research to identify new technologies and analytical methods that can be applied by partners to support critical infrastructure security and resilience efforts;
- Participating in the review and validation of critical infrastructure security and resilience risk analysis and management approaches; and
- Engaging and serving as a resource to local communities for efforts to enhance the security and resilience of physical and cyber critical infrastructure.

International Coordination

The nature of critical infrastructure ownership and operations is also distributed and the need for joint planning and investment is becoming more common and necessary on the international level.

These global connections inform the way that the critical infrastructure community should plan to work together, within and across sectors and across jurisdictions and national borders, to increase the security and resilience of critical infrastructure.

PPD-21 calls for international collaboration as part of the national unity of effort to strengthen security and resilience. To that end, Federal, private sector and international partners work together to implement coordinated global infrastructure security measures to protect against current and future physical and cyber threats.

International collaboration occurs in many areas, including

- Sharing information,
- Implementing existing agreements affecting critical infrastructure security and resilience,
- Developing policies for cross-border coordination of security and resilience initiatives,
- Addressing cross-sector and global issues such as cybersecurity and
- Enhancing understanding of cross-border interdependencies of critical infrastructure.

Information Sharing Among Sector Partners

Voluntary collaboration between private sector owners and operators (including their partner associations, vendors and others) and their government counterparts is the primary mechanism for advancing collective action toward national critical infrastructure security and resilience.

The effective implementation of the NIPP is predicated on active participation by government and private sector partners in robust, multidirectional information sharing.

- This enhances owners and operators ability to assess risks, make prudent security investments and develop appropriate resilience strategies.
- When the Government understands private sector information needs, it can adjust its information collection, analysis, synthesis and dissemination activities accordingly.
- When the private sector is assured that the critical infrastructure information that it shares with the government will be protected from release or disclosure, the Nation's critical infrastructure protection capabilities will be enhanced.

Benefits of Information Sharing

Information sharing enhances:

- Owners' and operators' ability to assess risks, make prudent security investments and develop appropriate resilience strategies.
- Government's ability to adjust its information collection, analysis, synthesis and dissemination activities based on the needs of the private sector.
- The critical infrastructure Information-Sharing Environment supports three levels of decisionmaking and action:
    - Strategic planning and investment
    - Situational awareness and preparedness
    - Operational planning and response

Information Flow and Decisionmaking

The NIPP information-sharing approach constitutes a shift from a strictly hierarchical to a networked model, allowing distribution and access to information to enable decentralized decisionmaking and actions.

The increasing availability of data and information essential to operating and maintaining infrastructure and related technologies enables more efficient and effective practices.

This information is vulnerable to unauthorized access that could affect its confidentiality, integrity, or availability. The distribution of such information to those entities that can use it for efficient and effective risk management remains a challenge.

Protecting Privacy, Civil Liberties and Critical Infrastructure Information

It is critical to maintain the availability of information and distribute it to those who can use and protect it properly. This entails being transparent about information-sharing practices; protecting sources and methods; and ensuring privacy and protecting civil liberties, while also enabling law enforcement investigations.

Supporting information-sharing initiatives exist both at the national and regional level. Information-sharing activities can protect privacy by applying the Fair

Information Practice Principles (FIPPs) and protect civil liberties by complying with applicable laws and policies.

It is equally crucial to ensure adequate protection of sensitive business and security information that could cause serious adverse impacts to private businesses, the economy and public or private enterprise security through unauthorized disclosure, access, or use.

The Federal Government has a statutory responsibility to safeguard critical infrastructure information.

DHS and other agencies use the Protected Critical Infrastructure Information (PCII) program and other protocols such as Classified National Security Information, Law Enforcement Sensitive Information and Federal Security Classification Guidelines.

The PCII program, authorized by the Critical Infrastructure Information (CII) Act of 2002 and its implementing regulations (Title 6 of the Code of Federal Regulations Part 29), defines both the requirements for submitting CII and those that government agencies must follow for accessing and safeguarding CII.

Safeguarding Against Unauthorized Disclosure and Access

NIPP implementation relies on the critical infrastructure information provided by the private sector and State, local, tribal, or territorial governments.

The NIPP recognizes that the disclosure of sensitive business or security information could cause serious damage to companies, the economy and public safety or security through unauthorized disclosure or access.

Protected Critical Infrastructure Information (PCII) Program

DHS and other Federal agencies use a number of programs and procedures, such as the Protected Critical Infrastructure Information (PCII) Program, to ensure that critical infrastructure information is properly safeguarded.

The PCII Program includes procedures that govern the receipt, validation, handling, dissemination, storage, marking and use of critical infrastructure information voluntarily submitted to the Department of Homeland Security. These procedures are also applicable to Federal, State, local, tribal, or territorial government employees or contractors supporting Federal agencies that have access to, handle, use, or store critical infrastructure information that enjoys protection under the Critical Infrastructure Information Act of 2002.

NIPP 2013 Supplement: Connecting to the NICC and the NCCIC

This supplement describes how partners throughout the critical infrastructure community can connect to the NICC and NCCIC. It describes the information desired by the centers and their partners, as well as how the centers protect and analyze data to inform prevention, protection, mitigation, response and recovery activities.

Presidential Policy Directive 21 (PPD-21) highlights the role of the national physical and cyber coordinating centers in enabling successful critical infrastructure security and resilience outcomes.

Presidential Policy Directive 41 (PPD-41) states that DHS, acting through the National Cybersecurity and Communications Integration Center (NCCIC), will serve as the lead Federal agency for (cybersecurity) asset response activities.

The National Infrastructure Coordinating Center (NICC) and the National Cybersecurity and Communications Integration Center (NCCIC) fulfill this Department of Homeland Security (DHS) responsibility within the critical infrastructure partnership.

Lesson 2 Summary

In this lesson you learned to:

- Describe the Risk Environment
- Identify dependencies and interdependencies across critical infrastructure systems
- Identify the relevant authorities and roles of:
    - The Department of Homeland Security (DHS).
    - Sector-Specific Agencies (SSAs).
    - Other Federal departments and agencies.
    - State, local, tribal and territorial jurisdictions.
    - Owners and operators.
- Discuss the importance of partnerships
- Describe the NIPP sector and cross-sector coordinating structure
- Describe how the NIPP fosters information sharing at all levels

Below are the NIPP 2013 resources referenced in this lesson for further review:

Lesson 3 Overview

Effective critical infrastructure protective programs and resilience strategies are comprehensive, coordinated, cost effective and risk-informed.

Risk management actions involve measures designed to prevent, deter and mitigate the threat; reduce vulnerability to an attack or other disaster; minimize consequences; and enable timely, efficient response and restoration.

This lesson provides an overview of the Collaborating to Implement the risk management framework. By the end of this lesson, you will be able to:

- Explain the elements of the risk management framework
- Describe how the risk management framework can be used to enhance critical infrastructure security and resilience within and across the critical infrastructure sectors.
- Identify activities incorporated in the risk management framework.

Managing Risk

Risk is influenced by the nature and magnitude of a threat, the vulnerabilities to that threat and the consequences that could result. Managing risks to critical infrastructure requires an integrated approach across this broad community to:

- Identify, deter, detect, disrupt and prepare for threats and hazards to the Nation's critical infrastructure;
- Reduce vulnerabilities of critical assets, systems and networks; and
- Mitigate the potential consequences to critical infrastructure of incidents or adverse events that do occur.

Given the diverse authorities, roles and responsibilities of critical infrastructure partners, flexible, proactive and inclusive partnerships are required to advance critical infrastructure security and resilience.

Risk

Glossary refers to the "potential for an unwanted outcome resulting from an incident, event, or occurrence, as determined by its likelihood [a function of threats and vulnerabilities] and the associated consequences."

Threat

Glossary A natural or manmade occurrence, individual, entity, or action that has or indicates the potential to harm life, information, operations, the environment and/or property.

Vulnerability

Glossary — A physical feature or operational attribute that renders an entity open to exploitation or susceptible to a given hazard.

Consequence

Glossary — The effect of an event, incident, or occurrence, including the number of deaths, injuries and other human health impacts along with economic impacts both direct and indirect and other negative outcomes to society.

Identifying Risks and Prioritizing Security Investments

The NIPP risk management framework establishes a process for identifying risks and prioritizing security and resilience initiatives and investments within and across sectors. The Strategic National Risk Assessment (SNRA), executed in support of PPD-8, helps identify the types of incidents that pose the greatest known threat to the Nation's homeland security, along with the uncertainty of potential interconnected events with unknown consequences.

The objective is to ensure that government and private sector resources are applied where they offer the most benefit for mitigating risk by lessening vulnerabilities, deterring threats and minimizing the consequences of all hazards, including terrorist attacks and other manmade and natural disasters.

Investments for ensuring security and resilience can include a wide range of activities, such as

- Hardening facilities, building resilience and redundancy and incorporating hazard resistance into facility design
- Initiating active or passive countermeasures installing security systems and implementing cybersecurity measures
- Promoting workforce surety programs, conducting training and exercises
- Planning for business continuity, including restoration and recovery actions

2011 Strategic National Risk Assessment (SNRA) National-Level Events

Threat/Hazard Group	Threat/Hazard Type	National-level Event Description
Natural	Animal Disease Outbreak	An unintentional introduction of the foot-and-mouth disease virus into the domestic livestock population in a U.S. state
Natural	Earthquake	An earthquake occurs within the U.S. resulting in direct economic losses greater than $100 Million
Natural	Flood	A flood occurs within the U.S. resulting in direct economic losses greater than $100 Million
Natural	Human Pandemic Outbreak	A severe outbreak of pandemic influenza with a 25% gross clinical attack rate spreads across the U.S. populace
Natural	Hurricane	A tropical storm or hurricane impacts the U.S. resulting in direct economic losses of greater than $100 Million
Natural	Space Weather	The sun emits bursts of electromagnetic radiation and energetic particles causing utility outages and damage to infrastructure
Natural	Tsunami	A tsunami with a wave of approximately 50 feet impacts the Pacific Coast of the U.S.
Natural	Volcanic Eruption	A volcano in the Pacific Northwest erupts impacting the surrounding areas with lava flows and ash and areas east with smoke and ash

Natural	Wildfire	A wildfire occurs within the U.S. resulting in direct economic losses greater than $100 Million
Technological/ Accidental	Biological Food Contamination	Accidental conditions where introduction of a biological agent (e.g., Salmonella, E. coli, botulinum toxin) into the food supply results in 100 hospitalizations or greater and a multi- state response
Technological/ Accidental	Chemical Substance Spill or Release	Accidental conditions where a release of a large volume of a chemical acutely toxic to human beings (a toxic inhalation hazard, or TIH) from a chemical plant, storage facility, or transportation mode results in either one or more offsite fatalities, or one or more fatalities (either on- or offsite) with offsite evacuations/shelter-in-place
Technological/ Accidental	Dam Failure	Accidental conditions where dam failure and inundation results in one fatality or greater
Technological/ Accidental	Radiological Substance Release	Accidental conditions where reactor core damage causes release of radiation
Adversarial/ Human-Caused	Aircraft as a Weapon	A hostile non-state actor(s) crashes a commercial or general aviation aircraft into a physical target within the U.S.
Adversarial/ Human-Caused	Armed Assault	A hostile non-state actor(s) uses assault tactics to conduct strikes on vulnerable target(s) within the U.S. resulting in at least one fatality or injury

Adversarial/ Human-Caused	Biological Terrorism Attack (non-food)	A hostile non-state actor(s) acquires, weaponizes and releases a biological agent against an outdoor, indoor, or water target, directed at a concentration of people within the U.S.
Adversarial/ Human-Caused	Chemical/ Biological Food Contamination Terrorism Attack	A hostile non-state actor(s) acquires, weaponizes and disperses a biological or chemical agent into food supplies within the U.S. supply chain
Adversarial/ Human-Caused	Chemical Terrorism Attack (non-food)	A hostile non-state actor(s) acquires, weaponizes and releases a chemical agent against an outdoor, indoor, or water target, directed at a concentration of people using an aerosol, ingestion, or dermal route of exposure
Adversarial/ Human-Caused	Cyber Attack against Data	A cyber-attack which seriously compromises the integrity or availability of data (the information contained in a computer system) or data processes resulting in economic losses of a Billion dollars or greater
Adversarial/ Human-Caused	Cyber Attack against Physical Infrastructure	An incident in which a cyber-attack is used as a vector to achieve effects which are beyond the computer (i.e., kinetic or other effects) resulting in one fatality or greater or economic losses of $100 Million or greater
Adversarial/ Human-Caused	Explosives Terrorism Attack	A hostile non-state actor(s) deploys a man-portable improvised explosive device (IED), Vehicle-borne IED, or Vessel IED in the U.S. against a concentration of people and/or structures

		such as critical commercial or government facilities, transportation targets, or critical infrastructure sites, etc., resulting in at least one fatality or injury
Adversarial/ Human-Caused	Nuclear Terrorism Attack	A hostile non-state actor(s) acquires an improvised nuclear weapon through manufacture from fissile material, purchase, or theft and detonates it within a major U.S. population center
Adversarial/ Human-Caused	Radiological Terrorism Attack	A hostile non-state actor(s) acquires radiological materials and disperses them through explosive or other means (e.g., a radiological dispersal device or RDD) or creates a radiation exposure device (RED)

Risk Management Framework

The cornerstone of the NIPP is its risk analysis and management framework. NIPP 2013 builds upon and updates the risk management framework.

This framework consists of several components, including three interwoven elements of critical infrastructure (physical, cyber and human) and five steps toward implementing the risk management framework.

The elements are integrated through information sharing feedback loop, as appropriate. In addition, this framework minimizes the number of steps or "chevrons" by including prioritization with the implementation of risk management activities.

Click on each chevron to access more information about these steps

Click on "Elements of Critical Infrastructure" or "Information Sharing Feedback Loop" for more information about these features of the risk management framework

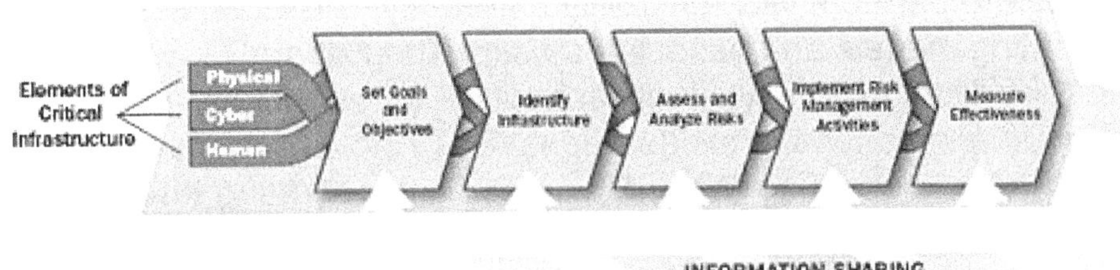

Set Infrastructure Goals and Objectives

This National Plan establishes a set of broad national goals for critical infrastructure security and resilience. These national goals are supported by objectives and priorities developed at the sector level, which may be articulated in Sector-Specific Plans (SSPs) and serve as targets for collaborative planning among SSAs and their sector partners in government and the private sector.

Sector-Specific Plans are:

- Tailored to address the unique perspective and risk landscape and methodologies and approaches associated with each sector.
- Developed jointly by the SSAs in close collaboration with Sector and Government Coordinating Councils (SCCs and GCCs) and others, including State, local, tribal and territorial critical infrastructure partners with key interests or expertise appropriate to the sector.

National Multi-Year Priorities:

Developed with input from all levels of the partnership, National multi-year priorities will complement these goals. These priorities might focus on particular goals or cross-sector issues where attention and resources could be applied within the critical infrastructure community with the most significant impact. Critical infrastructure owners and operators, as well as State, Local, Tribal, Territorial and regional entities, can identify objectives and priorities for critical infrastructure that align to these national priorities, national goals and sector objectives, but are tailored and scaled to their operational and risk environments and available resources.

Identify Infrastructure

To manage critical infrastructure risk effectively, partners must identify the assets, systems and networks that are essential to their continued operation, considering associated dependencies and interdependencies. This aspect of the risk management process also should identify information and communications technologies that facilitate the provision of essential services.

Critical infrastructure partners view criticality differently, based on their unique situations, operating models and associated risks. The Federal Government identifies and prioritizes nationally significant critical infrastructure based upon statutory definition and national considerations. SLTT governments identify and prioritize infrastructure according to their business and operating environments and associated risks. Infrastructure owners and operators identify assets, systems and networks that are essential to their continued operations and delivery of products and services to customers. At the sector level, many SSAs collaborate with owners and operators and SLTT entities to develop lists of infrastructure that are significant at the national, regional and local levels.

Effective risk management requires an understanding of criticality as well as the associated interdependencies of infrastructure. This National Plan identifies certain lifeline functions that are essential to the operation of most critical infrastructure sectors. These lifeline functions include communications, energy, transportation and water. Critical infrastructure partners should identify essential functions and resources that impact their businesses and communities. The identification of these lifeline functions can support preparedness planning and capability development.

Assess and Analyze Risks

Assess Risk

Risk is assessed as a function of consequence, vulnerability and threat. Consideration is given to the potential direct and indirect consequences of a terrorist attack or other hazards, known vulnerabilities to those threats or hazards and the nature and magnitude of the threat.

Critical infrastructure risks can be assessed in terms of the following:
- Threat – natural or manmade occurrence, individual, entity, or action that has or indicates the potential to harm life, information, operations, the environment and/or property.
- Vulnerability – physical feature or operational attribute that renders an entity open to exploitation or susceptible to a given hazard.
- Consequence – effect of an event, incident, or occurrence.

Risk assessments are conducted by many critical infrastructure partners to inform their own decisionmaking, using a broad range of methodologies. These assessments allow critical infrastructure community leaders to understand the most likely and severe incidents that could affect their operations and communities and use this information to support planning and resource allocation in a coordinated manner.

To assess risk effectively, critical infrastructure partners—including owners and operators, sector councils and government agencies—need timely, reliable and actionable information regarding threats, vulnerabilities and consequences. Non-governmental entities must be involved in the development and dissemination of products regarding threats, vulnerabilities and potential consequences and provide risk information in a trusted environment. Partners should understand intelligence and information requirements and conduct joint analysis where appropriate. Critical infrastructure partnerships can bring great value in improving the understanding of risk to both cyber and physical systems and assets. Neither public nor private sector entities can fully understand risk without this integration of wide-ranging knowledge and analysis.

Analyze Risk

Risk assessments are conducted on an asset, system, or network basis. Once the three components of risk—consequence, vulnerability and threat—have been assessed for one or more given assets, systems, or networks they must be integrated into a defensible model to produce a risk estimate. DHS has identified a number of risk assessment characteristics and data requirements to produce results that enable cross-sector risk comparisons; these are termed core criteria. These features provide a guide for improving or modifying existing methodologies as well as developing new ones.

Implement Risk Management Activities

Decision makers prioritize activities to manage critical infrastructure risk based on the criticality of the affected infrastructure, the costs of such activities and the potential for risk reduction. Some risk management activities address multiple aspects of risk, while others are more targeted to address specific threats, vulnerabilities, or potential consequences. These activities can be divided into the following approaches:

Identify, Deter, Detect, Disrupt and Prepare for Threats and Hazards

- Establish and implement joint plans and processes to evaluate needed increases in security and resilience measures, based on hazard warnings and threat reports.
- Conduct continuous monitoring of cyber systems.
- Employ security protection systems to detect or delay an attack or intrusion.
- Detect malicious activities that threaten critical infrastructure and related operational activities across the sectors.

- Implement intrusion detection or intrusion protection systems on sensitive or mission-critical networks and facilities to identify and prevent unauthorized access and exploitation.
- Monitor critical infrastructure facilities and systems potentially targeted for attack (e.g., through local law enforcement and public utilities).

Reduce Vulnerabilities

- Build security and resilience into the design and operation of assets, systems and networks.
- Employ siting considerations when locating new infrastructure, such as avoiding floodplains, seismic zones and other risk-prone locations.
- Develop and conduct training and exercise programs to enhance awareness and understanding of common vulnerabilities and possible mitigation strategies.
- Leverage lessons learned and apply corrective actions from incidents and exercises to enhance protective measures.
- Establish and execute business and government emergency action and continuity plans at the local and regional levels to facilitate the continued performance of critical functions during an emergency.
- Address cyber vulnerabilities through continuous diagnostics and prioritization of high-risk vulnerabilities.
- Undertake research and development efforts to reduce known cyber and physical vulnerabilities that have proved difficult or expensive to address.

Mitigate Consequences

- Share information to support situational awareness and damage assessments of cyber and physical critical infrastructure during and after an incident, including the nature and extent of the threat, cascading effects and the status of the response.
- Work to restore critical infrastructure operations following an incident.
- Support the provision of essential services such as: emergency power to critical facilities; fuel supplies for emergency responders; and potable water, mobile communications and food and pharmaceuticals for the affected community.
- Ensure that essential information is backed up on remote servers and that redundant processes are implemented for key functions, reducing the potential consequences of a cybersecurity incident.
- Remove key operational functions from the Internet-connected business network, reducing the likelihood that a cybersecurity incident will result in compromise of essential services.
- Ensure that incidents affecting cyber systems are fully contained; that asset, system, or network functionality is restored to pre-incident status;

and that affected information is available in an uncompromised and
secure state.
- Recognize and account for interdependencies in response and
recovery/restoration plans.
- Repair or replace damaged infrastructure with cost-effective designs
that are more secure and resilient.
- Utilize and ensure the reliability of emergency communications
capabilities.
- Contribute to the development and execution of private sector, SLTT
and regional priorities for both near- and long-term recovery.

The above activities are examples of risk management activities that are being
undertaken to support the overall achievement of security and resilience,
whether at an organizational, community, sector, or national level.

The Prioritization Process

The prioritization process, now incorporated into the Implement Risk
Management Activities step of the NIPP risk management framework, involves
aggregating, combining and analyzing risk assessment results to determine
which assets, systems, networks, sectors, or combinations of these face the
highest risk so that risk management priorities can be established.

It also provides the basis for understanding potential risk-mitigation benefits
that are used to inform planning and resource decisions.

The NIPP risk management framework provides the process for developing
comparable estimates of the risk relevant to critical infrastructure.

Comparing the risk faced by different entities helps identify where risk
mitigation is needed and to subsequently determine and help justify the most
cost-effective risk management options.

In addition, this prioritization process develops information that can be used
during incident response to help inform decision makers regarding issues
associated with critical infrastructure restoration.

Measure Effectiveness

While the results of risk analyses help set national and sector priorities,
performance metrics allow NIPP partners to track progress against these
priorities. The metrics provide a basis to establish accountability, document
actual performance, facilitate diagnoses, promote effective management and
provide a feedback mechanism to decision makers.

The critical infrastructure community evaluates the effectiveness of risk management efforts within sectors and at national, State, local and regional levels by developing metrics for both direct and indirect indicator measurement. SSAs work with SCCs through the sector-specific planning process to develop attributes that support the national goals and national priorities as well as other sector-specific priorities. Such measures inform the risk management efforts of partners throughout the critical infrastructure community and help build a national picture of progress toward the vision of this National Plan as well as the National Preparedness Goal. At a national level, the National Plan articulates broad area goals to achieve the Plan's vision that will be complemented by a set of multi-year national priorities. The critical infrastructure community will subsequently evaluate its collective progress in accomplishing the goals and priorities.

This evaluation process functions as an integrated and continuing cycle:
- Articulate the vision and national goals;
- Define national priorities;
- Identify high-level outputs or outcomes associated with the national goals and national priorities;
- Collect performance data to assess progress in achieving identified outputs and outcomes;
- Evaluate progress toward achievement of the national priorities, national goals and vision;
- Update the national priorities and adapt risk management activities accordingly; and
- Revisit the national goals and vision on a periodic basis.

Just as regular evaluation of progress toward the national goals informs the ongoing evolution of security and resilience practices, planned exercises and real-world incidents also provide opportunities for learning and adaptation.

For example, fuel shortages after Hurricane Sandy illustrated the interdependencies and complexities of infrastructure systems, the challenges in achieving shared situational awareness during large events and the need for improved information collection and sharing among government and private sector partners to support restoration activities.

The critical infrastructure and national preparedness communities also conduct exercises on an ongoing basis through the National Exercise Program and other mechanisms to assess and validate the capabilities of organizations, agencies and jurisdictions.

During and after such planned and unplanned operations, partners identify individual and group weaknesses, implement and evaluate corrective actions and share best practices with the wider critical infrastructure and emergency management communities.

Such learning and adaptation inform future plans, activities, technical assistance, training and education.

NIPP Performance Management

The key to NIPP performance management is to align outcome metrics to sector priorities. The 16 sectors are diverse, operate in every State and affect every level of government. As a result, NIPP priorities and many NIPP metrics will vary from sector to sector. All NIPP metrics must be specific and clear as to what they are measuring, practical or feasible in that the needed data are available and built on objectively measured data.

Measuring Performance

In addition to outcome metrics, other information will be utilized, such as output data and descriptive data.

Output (or Process) Data are used to gauge whether specific activities were performed as planned, track the progress of a task, or report on the output of a process. Output data show progress toward performing the activities necessary to achieve critical infrastructure protection goals and can serve as leading indicators for outcome measures. They also help build a comprehensive picture of critical infrastructure security status and activities. Examples include the number of protective programs implemented in a fiscal year, percentage of sector organizations exchanging critical infrastructure information and the level of response to a data call for asset information.

Descriptive Data are used to understand sector resources and activities, but do not reflect critical infrastructure security performance. Examples include: a narrative description of progress; the number of facilities in a jurisdiction; the population resident or working in the area affected by an incident; and the number of suppliers in an infrastructure service provider's supply chain. NIPP metrics are evolving from the current focus on descriptive and output data to a focus on outcome metrics. Descriptive and output data have been critical during the initial implementation of the NIPP in order to closely track the progress of the sectors in building key NIPP elements, such as the SSPs and GCCs/SCCs. The next stage of NIPP implementation will concentrate on working with the sectors to identify and track outcome metrics that are aligned to sector priorities and provide NIPP partners with a more comprehensive assessment of the success of critical infrastructure security efforts.

Gathering Performance Information DHS works with the SSAs and sector partners to:

- Gather the information necessary to measure the level of performance associated with the progress indicators. Given the inherent differences in critical infrastructure sectors, a "one size fits all" approach to gathering this information is not appropriate.
- Determine the appropriate measurement approach to be included in the sector's SSP.
- Ensure that partners engaged with multiple sectors or in cross-sector matters are not subject to unnecessary redundancy or conflicting guidance in information collection.

Information collected as part of this effort is protected. Information collected as part of this effort is protected.

Assessing Performance and Reporting on Progress

The National Critical Infrastructure Annual Report:

- Is based on information about priorities, requirements and related program funding information that is submitted to DHS by the SSA of each sector, the SLTTGCC and the RC3.
- Analyzes information about sector priorities, requirements and programs in the context of the National Risk Profile, a high-level summary of the aggregate risk and protective status of all sectors.

The National Risk Profile:

- Drives the development of national priorities, which, in turn, are used to assess existing critical infrastructure programs and to identify existing gaps or shortfalls in national critical infrastructure security efforts.
- Provides the Executive Office of the President with information that supports both strategic and investment decisions related to critical infrastructure security and resilience.

Physical, Cyber and Human Elements

The three interwoven elements of critical infrastructure (physical, cyber and human) are explicitly identified and should be integrated throughout the steps of the framework, as appropriate.

The risk management framework is comprehensive and takes into account the assets, systems and networks that include one or more of the following elements:

- Physical — tangible property
- Cyber — electronic information and communications systems and the information contained therein

- Human — critical knowledge of functions or people uniquely susceptible to attack

Information Sharing Loop

The framework now depicts the importance of information sharing throughout the entire risk management process. Information is shared through each step of the framework, to include the "measure effectiveness" step, facilitating feedback and enabling continuous improvement of critical infrastructure security and resilience efforts.

Qualitative Feedback

The NIPP provides mechanisms for qualitative feedback that can be applied to augment and improve the effectiveness and efficiency of public and private sector critical infrastructure protective programs and resilience strategies.

DHS works with sector partners to identify and share lessons learned and best practices for all aspects of the risk management process. DHS also works with SSAs to share relevant input from sector partners and other sources that can be used as part of the national effort to continuously improve critical infrastructure security and resilience.

Risk Management Framework Features

The critical infrastructure risk management framework is designed to provide flexibility for use in all sectors, across different geographic regions and by various partners. It can be tailored to dissimilar operating environments and applies to all threats and hazards.

The framework supports a collaborative decisionmaking process to inform the selection of risk management actions.

Many organizations have risk management models that have proved effective and should be maintained, however, this framework provides an organizing construct for those models.

The risk management framework:
- Is applicable to threats such as disasters, manmade safety hazards and terrorism.
- Integrates and coordinates strategies, capabilities and governance to enable risk-informed decisionmaking.

- Is tailored and applied on an asset, system, network, or functional basis, depending on the fundamental characteristics of the individual critical infrastructure sectors.

Risk Reduction

In addition to the identified threat-, vulnerability- and consequence-reducing activities, risk reduction can be achieved through critical infrastructure and control system design.

Factoring security and resilience measures into design decisions early can facilitate integration of measures to mitigate physical and cyber vulnerabilities as well as natural and technological hazards at lower cost.

Governments and businesses can better invest in measures that increase the security and resilience of both critical infrastructure and the broader society through risk analysis, evidence-based design practices and consideration of costs and benefits.

Such efforts are also helpful during infrastructure recovery efforts, in those instances when the Federal Government is working with communities and industry to rebuild infrastructure.

NIPP 2013 Supplement: National Protection and Programs Directorate Resources to Support Vulnerability Assessments

Assessing vulnerabilities of critical infrastructure is an important step in developing security solutions and managing critical infrastructure risk. The Department of Homeland Security's (DHS) National Protection and Programs Directorate (NPPD) works with owners and operators to conduct vulnerability assessments of select critical infrastructure to inform its internal risk management processes and provide technical assistance to its State, local, tribal and territorial (SLTT) and private sector partners to enable their own risk assessments and security plans. NPPD provides additional resources, typically in the form of informational material on known vulnerabilities, to help owners and operators understand vulnerabilities at a more general level.

This supplement provides information on Federal resources that are used by DHS and available to SLTT governments and critical infrastructure owners and operators to identify and assess critical infrastructure vulnerabilities.

NIPP 2013 Supplement: Incorporating Resilience into Critical Infrastructure Projects

This supplement provides the steps that support development decisions and investments in infrastructure that will enhance the resilience of critical infrastructure systems. This supplement was developed through research into existing resilience strategies, including the Hurricane Sandy Rebuilding Strategy and the updated NIPP 2013, Partnering for Critical Infrastructure Security and Resilience.

It is intended for government decision makers at all levels who are undertaking new infrastructure projects or enhancing security and mitigation measures on existing government-owned infrastructure. It also can be used more broadly by all critical infrastructure owners and operators as decisions are made to invest in infrastructure replacements or improvements.

NIPP 2013 Supplement: Executing a Critical Infrastructure Risk Management Approach

Risk information allows partners to prioritize risk management efforts.

This supplement describes a useful critical infrastructure risk management approach which supports the risk management framework. The framework enables the integration of related critical infrastructure strategies, capabilities and governance structures to enable risk-informed decisionmaking. The risk management approach described in this supplement can be applied to all threats and hazards, although different information and methodologies may be used to understand each.

Lesson 3 Summary

In this lesson you learned to:
- Explain the elements of the risk management framework
- Describe how the risk management framework can be used to enhance critical infrastructure security and resilience within and across the critical infrastructure sectors.
- Identify activities incorporated in the risk management framework.

Below are the NIPP 2013 resources referenced in this lesson for further review:

Lesson 4 Overview

This lesson provides an overview of the Call to Action: Steps to Advance the National Effort. By the end of this lesson, you will be able to:

- Describe actions critical infrastructure community partners can take to:

    o Build upon partnership efforts

    o Innovate in managing risk

    o Focus on outcomes
- Explain how these actions inform and guide priority-setting and joint planning efforts

Call to Action: Steps to Advance the National Effort

NIPP 2013 envisions a Nation in which physical and cyber critical infrastructure remain secure and resilient, with vulnerabilities reduced, consequences minimized, threats identified and disrupted and response and recovery hastened. It provides a clear call to action to leverage partnerships, innovate in risk management and focus on outcomes.

The NIPP Call to Action is meant to guide the collaborative efforts of the critical infrastructure community to advance security and resilience outcomes under three broad activity categories:

- Build upon Partnership Efforts
- Innovate in Managing Risk
- Focus on Outcomes

Federal departments and agencies, engaging with State, Local, Tribal, Territorial, regional and private sector partners—taking into consideration the unique risk management perspectives, priorities and resource constraints of each sector—will work together to promote continuous improvement of security and resilience efforts to accomplish the tasks called for.

A Complete List of the Calls to Action

The Call to Action calls upon the critical infrastructure community (respective of authorities, responsibilities and business environments) to take cross-cutting, proactive and coordinated actions that support collective efforts to strengthen critical infrastructure security and resilience in the coming years.

Build upon Partnership Efforts:

1. Set National Focus through Jointly-Developed Priorities

2. Determine Collective Actions through Joint-Planning Efforts
3. Empower Local and Regional Partnerships to Build Capacity Nationally
4. Leverage Incentives to Advance Security and Resilience

Innovate in Managing Risk:

5. Enable Risk-Informed Decision-making through Enhanced Situational Awareness
6. Analyze Infrastructure Dependencies, Interdependencies and Associated Cascading Effects
7. Identify, Assess and Respond to Unanticipated Infrastructure Cascading Effects During and Following Incidents
8. Promote Infrastructure, Community and Regional Recovery Following Incidents
9. Strengthen Coordinated Development and Delivery of Technical Assistance, Training and Education
10. Improve Critical Infrastructure Security and Resilience by Advancing Research and Development Solutions

Focus on Outcomes:

11. Evaluate Progress toward the Achievement of Goals
12. Learn and Adapt During and After Exercises and Incidents

Links between Call to Action, Risk Management Framework and National Goals

Throughout NIPP 2013, call-out boxes identify linkages between the Call to Action activities, steps toward implementing the risk management framework and the National Goals covered earlier in this course.

The National Goals include:

1. Assess and analyze risks to critical infrastructure
2. Address the human, physical and cyber threat
3. Enhance security and resilience through advance planning
4. Share actionable and relevant information across the critical infrastructure community
5. Promote learning and adaptation

Five steps toward implementing the risk management framework include:

1. Set Infrastructure Goals and Objectives
2. Identify Infrastructure
3. Assess and Analyze Risks
4. Implement Risk Management Activities
5. Measure Effectiveness

What SLTT Executives Can Do

The NIPP calls on executive decisionmakers in the private sector and elected officials at the State, Local, Tribal and Territorial (SLTT) level to work with partners across the critical infrastructure community to manage risks and achieve security and resilience outcomes.

Build Upon Partnership Efforts

- Foster active local and regional cross-sector partnerships.
- Evaluate your organization's risk management policies with the NIPP framework.
- Engage private sector partners in your area of responsibility on critical infrastructure security and resilience efforts.
- Use existing partnership structures to enhance relationships across the critical infrastructure community.
- Encourage staff attendance in webinars, conference calls, cross-sector events and listening sessions.

Innovate in Managing Risk

- Identify the strengths and weaknesses in your organization's security posture and explore the government and industry resources available to improve.
- Consider security and resilience when designing infrastructure.
- Encourage private sector and emergency response coordination on emergency management plans and exercises.
- Share essential security and resilience information with partners.
- Review and use the Cybersecurity Framework.
- Participate in the Critical Infrastructure Cyber Community (C³) voluntary program.
- Use training and exercises to innovate and evaluate critical infrastructure security and resilience.
- Encourage staff attendance in risk management trainings.
- Promote risk management across the state.
- Encourage information sharing within the state and with neighboring States.

Focus on Outcomes

- Participate in critical infrastructure planning and priority setting activities.
- Identify effective security and resilience practices.
- Understand interdependencies.
- Share success stories and opportunities for improvement with critical infrastructure partners.

What Private Sector Companies Can Do

The NIPP outlines how government and private sector participants in the critical infrastructure community work together to manage risks and achieve security and resilience outcomes.

Build Upon Partnership Efforts

- Become involved in sector-specific and information sharing partnerships
- Establish relationships with key local partners including emergency management
- Participate in training and exercises; Attend webinars, conference calls, cross-sector events and listening sessions.

Innovate in Managing Risk

- Incorporate security and resilience into the design and upkeep of critical infrastructure
- Help develop analysis to better understand risks
- Adopt the Cybersecurity Framework.

Focus on Outcomes

- Identify shared goals, define success and document effective practices.
- Build security and resilience considerations into cost-benefit analysis to understand return on investment

What First Responder Organizations Can Do

The NIPP calls on State and Local Law Enforcement, Fusion Centers and Public Safety organizations to work with State, Local, Tribal and Territorial government and private sector partners across the critical infrastructure community to manage risks and achieve security and resilience outcomes.

Build Upon Partnership Efforts

- Become involved in a relevant local, regional sector and cross-sector partnership.
- Engage with private sector partners in your area of responsibility on critical infrastructure security and resilience efforts.
- Use existing partnership structures to enhance relationships across the critical infrastructure community.

Innovate in Managing Risk

- Work with private sector and emergency response partners on emergency management plans and exercising participation and response.
- Participate in multi-directional information sharing.
- Review and use the Cybersecurity Framework.
- Use training and exercises to innovate and evaluate critical infrastructure security and resilience.

Focus on Outcomes

- Participate in critical infrastructure planning and priority setting activities.
- Participate in implementation efforts.
- Identify effective security and resilience practices.
- Understand interdependencies.
- Share success stories and opportunities for improvement.

Lesson 4 Summary

In this lesson you learned to:
- Describe actions critical infrastructure community partners can take to:
    - Build upon partnership efforts
    - Innovate in managing risk
    - Focus on outcomes
- Explain how these actions inform and guide priority-setting and joint planning efforts

Below are the NIPP 2013 resources referenced in this lesson for further review:

Course Summary

Throughout this course, you were introduced to the National Infrastructure Protection Plan (NIPP). As you have learned, implementing critical infrastructure security and resilience requires partnerships, coordination and collaboration among all levels of government and the private sector.

Course Objectives:

- Describe NIPP 2013 key concepts across the entire critical infrastructure community — including private sector and government at all levels.
- Describe the core tenets as the values and assumptions considered when planning for critical infrastructure security and resilience
- Identify activities critical partners may implement to achieve national goals aimed at enhancing critical infrastructure security and resilience put forward in the NIPP 2013 Call to Action
- Describe ways to apply these concepts to support security and resilience within your community or area of responsibility

Resources

- <u>National Infrastructure Protection Plan 2013: Partnering for Critical Infrastructure Security and Resilience</u>
- NIPP 2013 Supplements
    - <u>Connecting to the NICC and the NCCIC</u>
    - <u>Executing a Critical Infrastructure Risk Management Approach</u>
    - <u>Incorporating Resilience into Critical Infrastructure Projects</u>
    - <u>National Protection and Programs Directorate Resources to Support Vulnerability Assessments</u>
- Sector-Specific Plans
- <u>Homeland Security Act of 2002</u>
- <u>Presidential Policy Directive 8 (PPD-8): National Preparedness (2011)</u>
- <u>Presidential Policy Directive 21 (PPD-21): Critical Infrastructure Security and Resilience (2013)</u>
- <u>Presidential Policy Directive 41 (PPD-41): United States Cyber Incident Coordination (2016)</u>
- <u>Executive Order 13636: Improving Critical Infrastructure Cybersecurity (2013)</u>
- <u>National Preparedness Goal and System</u>

- <u>National Planning Frameworks for each of the five preparedness mission areas</u>
- <u>President's Climate Action Plan (2013)</u>
- <u>National Strategy for Information Sharing and Safeguarding (2013)</u>
- <u>Strategic National Risk Assessment (SNRA)</u>
- <u>Joint National Priorities</u>
- National Critical Infrastructure Annual Report
- National Risk Profile

For more information about other critical infrastructure resources, go to <u>www.dhs.gov/critical-infrastructure-resources</u>

Follow-on Training

For more in-depth information about the topics covered in this course, consider taking these independent study courses

- IS-913: Achieving Results through Critical Infrastructure Partnerships and Collaboration
- IS-921: Implementing Critical Infrastructure Protection Programs
- IS-915: Protecting Critical Infrastructure against Insider Threats
- IS-454: Fundamentals of Risk Management
- IS-800: National Response Framework
- IS-821: Introduction to the Critical Infrastructure Support Annex